Isadora Dances

by Rachel Isadora

VIKING

VIKING
Published by the Penguin Group
Penguin Putnam Inc., 375 Hudson Street, New York, New York 10014, U.S.A.
Penguin Books Ltd, 27 Wrights Lane, London W8 5TZ, England
Penguin Books Australia Ltd, Ringwood, Victoria, Australia
Penguin Books Canada Ltd, 10 Alcorn Avenue, Toronto, Ontario, Canada M4V 3B2
Penguin Books (N.Z.) Ltd, 182-190 Wairau Road, Auckland 10, New Zealand

Penguin Books Ltd, Registered Offices: Harmondsworth, Middlesex, England

First published in 1998 by Viking, a member of Penguin Putnam Inc.

1 3 5 7 9 10 8 6 4 2

LIBRARY OF CONGRESS CATALOGING-IN-PUBLICATION DATA
Isadora, Rachel.
Isadora dances / by Rachel Isadora.
p. cm.
Includes bibliographical references (p.).
Summary: A brief biography of the woman whose unique style of dance was not
readily accepted by audiences at the turn of the twentieth century.
ISBN 0-670-87893-6
1. Duncan, Isadora, 1877–1927—Juvenile literature. 2. Dancers—United
States—Biography—Juvenile literature. [1. Duncan, Isadora, 1877–1927.
2. Dancers. 3. Women—Biography.] I. Title.
GV1785.D8I73 1998 792.8′092—dc21 [B] 97-27294 CIP AC

Printed in China   Set in Perpetua

The quotations in *Isadora Dances* are taken from Isadora Duncan's
autobiography, *My Life*.

For my mother

𝒯he Chopin waltz was beautiful. Isadora could not sit still. Evenings were a special time for Augustine, Elizabeth, Raymond, and Isadora, when their mother, Dora, played the piano or recited poetry. Sometimes the children would dance until morning. "This was my real education," Isadora said. "These hours were to us enchanted." Isadora, born in 1877, was the youngest of the four children.

On occasion, a close friend of Dora's would join the Duncans for the evening and watch in delight as Isadora composed lovely dances. She was reminded of the famous ballerina Fanny Elssler. At Dora's friend's urging, Isadora was brought for ballet lessons. "When the teacher told me to stand on my toes I asked him why, and when he replied, 'Because it is beautiful,' I said that it was ugly and against nature and after the third lesson I left his class, never to return."

One day Dora came home and found that Isadora had collected half a dozen babies from their San Francisco neighborhood, all of them too young to walk. They were sitting on the floor while Isadora was teaching them to wave their arms. When Dora asked what this was all about, Isadora explained that this was her "school of dance." Before long, little girls from the neighborhood were coming and their parents were paying for them to take lessons. By the time Isadora was ten years old her classes were very popular and had grown quite large.

"I dreamed of a different dance," Isadora said. "My art was already in me when I was a little girl." Isadora believed that true dance came from the soul, untouched and free, unlike the dance she saw, where you were told what to do, how to pose, what to wear. "My ideas on the dance were to express the feelings and emotions of humanity. I was not at all interested in fairies," she said.

Isadora wanted to share her new kind of dance. At seventeen years old she left home. Everywhere she went people said, "It's lovely, but not for the theater." After months of auditions, she joined a touring theater group based in New York City. Though she did wind up dancing a fairy after all, in *A Midsummer Night's Dream*, it was in her own style, and the audience loved her. The manager was furious. He did not want dance to be the hit of his play. From then on, every time Isadora danced, he had the lights turned off. "Nobody could see anything on the stage but a white fluttering thing," Isadora said. After two years of hard work and little pay she left.

Isadora gave recitals to help earn much-needed money for her family. Word spread about the exotic young dancer, and soon everyone wanted to see her. During one concert, when Isadora appeared before the audience, forty women instantly got up and left in a huff. They were shocked. The filmy material Isadora had draped around her body made her appear almost naked! Women of the day were always covered from head to toe. Even dancers wore long costumes, silk tights, and corsets.

In May 1899, the Duncans left for England. Isadora felt it was time to show the world her dance. One summer night, while Isadora and her brother Raymond were dancing in Kensington Gardens, a London park, a beautiful woman in a large black hat saw them and asked, "Where on earth did you people come from?"

"Not from the earth at all," Isadora replied, "but from the moon."

"Well," the lady said, "whether from the earth or the moon, you are very sweet; won't you come and see me?" The lady was a famous actress, Mrs. Patrick Campbell, who, after seeing Isadora dance, introduced her to her wealthy friends. Soon, Isadora was invited to give recitals all the time.

After London, Isadora toured many countries. Everywhere she went, she was a sensation. Everything about Isadora was different: the way she looked, the way she moved, the way she lived. It was all so new and exciting to the people who saw her; she changed the way they thought forever.

On only one occasion, Isadora danced on stage with a corps de ballet. She whirled barefoot as they turned and balanced on point. But the two very different forms of dance did not work together. Isadora decided that the next time she shared a stage, it would be with dancers she had trained in her own style. She would start her own school.

Hundreds of parents brought their children to audition at
Isadora's yellow house. She chose only twenty little girls, ages
four to eight, to be her first pupils. The children wore the same
"uniform" as Isadora, a tunic and sandals. They lived at the yellow

house, where they were taught dance, music, art, and academic
subjects. There was no tuition, as Isadora planned to support the
school through her many performances.

Isadora's students became known as the "Isadorables." They performed with Isadora, always wearing flowing tunics. Audiences loved them, and soon dance schools opened teaching the new style. Even traditional schools adopted Isadora's original way of moving. Bare feet were becoming as acceptable as toe shoes.

Isadora had two children who were the joy of her life. As they were returning home from lunch in Paris one spring day, the automobile carrying six-year-old Deirdre, three-year-old Patrick, and their nanny stalled. The driver got out to crank it up. Suddenly, the car jumped to life and began to roll toward the river Seine. Unable to catch up with it, the driver watched in horror as it plunged into the water. By the time the police arrived, the children and their nanny had drowned. Isadora received thousands of letters and words of love from people all over the world who mourned the deaths of little Deirdre and Patrick. She could no longer dance.

As time passed, Isadora knew
she must dance again. She
danced her great sorrow, and as
always the audience loved her.
She wrote that love from
friends all over the world
"helped me to realize what
alone could comfort me—that
all men are my brothers, all
women my sisters, and all little
children on earth my children."

Isadora was fifty years old, long after most dancers stop dancing, when she gave a concert in Paris. She was cheered and called back to the stage again and again. Needing to rest after the concert, she went to visit friends in the south of France. Suddenly, on September 14, 1927, Isadora was killed in an automobile accident.

1877–1927

Angela Dora (Isadora) Duncan would not conform to the ideas of the world she lived in. Eventually that world came to understand Isadora, and *it* changed. Today, the spirit of Isadora lives, not only in dance but in all the arts.